Zeke and the Flute

By Sally Cowan

It is very hot.

Zeke the snake slides up the sand dune.

Zeke spots Pete the mule.

"Will you be my pal, dude?" said Zeke.

But Pete is not happy to see Zeke.

Zeke slides up to a tent.
He spots a long tube
on the sand.

But the tube is mute.
It will not chat with Zeke.

The tube is not a cute snake.

It is a flute!

"Hand me my flute, Steve!" said Jude.

Jude plays some tunes.

Steve swings to the tunes.

Steve spots Zeke.

“That snake likes these tunes!” said Steve.

Zeke did not make a pal,
but he had a fun time.

He slides off into the dunes.

CHECKING FOR MEANING

1. What does Zeke want to find? *(Literal)*
2. What does Zeke see on the sand? *(Literal)*
3. Do you think Pete the mule liked Zeke? Why? *(Inferential)*

EXTENDING VOCABULARY

dune	What is a dune? Where do you find dunes? What is another word you could use for *dune*?
mule	What type of animal is a mule? What other animals are similar to a mule?
mute	What does the word *mute* mean? Why was the tube on the sand mute?

MOVING BEYOND THE TEXT

1. Do you like snakes? Why?
2. How do snakes move? How do mules move?
3. Where else can you find snakes? What should you do if you see a snake?
4. Do you know how to play a musical instrument? Which one? If not, what instrument would you like to learn to play?

TIME TO WRITE

Imagine that Zeke finds a new friend after all. Write about how he meets the new friend.

PRACTICE WORDS

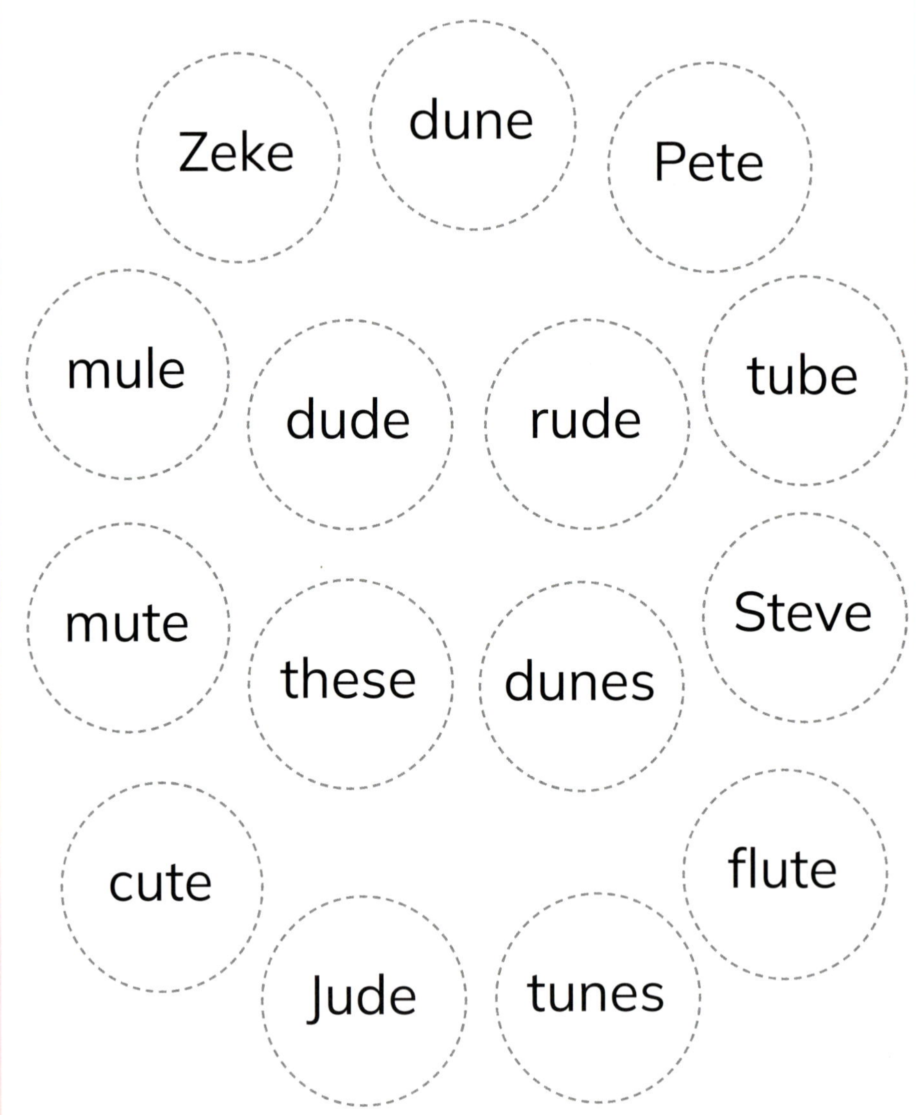